Professor Birdsong's

177

DUMBEST ROGUES

Thieves, Thugs & Rogues Series: Book Three

Leonard Birdsong

Winghurst Publications

Professor Birdsong's 177 Dumbest Rogues by Leonard Birdsong
© 2020 Leonard Birdsong

ISBN: 978-0-9979573-6-5 (Paperback)
ISBN: 978-0-9979573-7-2 (Kindle)

Winghurst Publications
1969 S. Alafaya Trail / Suite 303
Orlando, FL 32828-8732
www.BirdsongsLaw.com
lbirdsong22@gmail.com

Permissions:

Cover graphics: ©Khalid S. Birdsong /
http:friedchickenandsushi.com

Book cover design: Rik Feeney /
www.RickFeeney.com

Table of Contents

Table of Contents 3

Preface to Book Three.. 5

Introduction 7

CHAPTER 1 9

Rogues of The East Coast

CHAPTER 2 15

A Bushel Basket full of Pennsylvania Rogues

CHAPTER 3 23

Florida Rogues on Parade

CHAPTER 4 39

A Bunch of Rogues from The Old South

CHAPTER 5 49

A Few Mid-West Rogues

CHAPTER 6 57

Rogues from Texas & The West

CHAPTER 7 63

Rogues of California & The Pacific Coast

CHAPTER 8... 69

We End With Rogues from Abroad

About the Author.. 87

Ordering Information.. 89

Books by Professor Birdsong:................................. 91

Preface to Book Three

177 DUMBEST ROGUES

Although many people cannot define the word rogue, most people know a rogue when they meet one. The word rogue is defined as a dishonest or unprincipled man. Another definition of a rogue is that of a person whose behavior one disapproves of but who is nonetheless likable or attractive. Finally, a rogue is also defined as a person or thing that behaves in an aberrant, faulty or unpredictable way.

You will find many rogues in this chapter that certainly fit this final definition because such people act in dumb, aberrant ways that are often faulty and/or very unpredictable in their ways.

Enjoy!

Introduction

Law Professor Leonard Birdsong lives in Florida where he has taught Criminal Law, Evidence, and Immigration Law. He has written many scholarly legal pieces since joining the legal academy. This is not one of those scholarly pieces!

This trilogy series of Professor Birdsong's newest *Dumbest Criminal Stories: Thieves, Thugs & Rogues* is written just for fun and enjoyment. It showcases stories from all over the world and contains the k i n d of m a n y d u m b , funny and weird criminal law stories that he has found and written about since 2008. Read them. Laugh at the stories and then go to Amazon.com and choose from his other inexpensive fourteen humor books for more such laughs.

CHAPTER 1

Rogues of the East Coast

NEW YORK: *Does Batman know about this?* We learn that an upstate bandit robbed a bank carrying an umbrella and dressed as the villain The Penguin. The man allegedly strolled into a Trustco Bank in the town of Wappinger wearing a ski mask and carrying an open umbrella. He threatened to blow up the bank if he was let into the bank vault. He made off with an undisclosed amount of cash.

NEW YORK CITY: *The headline – "Jail for jailhouse sales gal."* A long-time corrections officer who ran a "Jailhouse Shopping Network" that supplied Manhattan inmates with everything from drugs to cigarettes, phones and pliers was sentenced to six years behind bar at the end of April, 2016. Patricia Howard, 44, was sentenced for scheming with an inmate and his niece, gouging prisoners up to $100 for a pack of cigarettes. Ms. Howard was charged with promoting prison contraband while working at the downtown Manhattan Detention Center known as the Tombs between December 2014 and May 2015.

NEW YORK CITY: *"Woes of the fat felon…"* William "Wobbles" Soler, a 500-pound accused gunrunner, was back in court recently but had major problems fitting into the courthouse elevators and, even briefly shutting down a courtroom because of his size. Wobbles and his extra-wide wheelchair could not fit into the inmate-transport elevators of the courthouse, so he was hoisted by way of the freight elevator to his 15th scheduled Bronx court appearance for allegedly leading a crew that sold 93 guns to undercover police officers. Once in the courtroom Wobbles had to remain on the audience side of the courtroom. Why? His wheelchair was too wide to reach the defense table. When it was time for him to confer with his lawyers about a possible pleas deal, the courtroom had to be completely cleared of others in order that he could have privacy to confer with his lawyer. There is no immediate follow up news as to whether a plea deal had been accepted. This was in May 2016.

NEW YORK: *ISIS IDIOT!!* A Rochester pizzeria owner who admitted he tried to recruit people for ISIS was sentenced in March 2106 to 22 ½ years in prison. Mufid Elfgeeh, who owned a convenience store and pizza shop, had pleaded guilty in November 2015 to attempting to provide material support to a terrorist organization. Authorities contend he tried to recruit three people to join ISIS to fight in Syria. According to court filings, Elfgeeh has renounced ISIS since his arrest.

NEW YORK CITY: *Idiot ammo arrest.* A suspected gang member was caught and arrested for trying to smuggle a fully loaded assault-rifle clip into a Bronx courthouse. In mid-May 2019, Isaiah Brown was on his way to the courthouse for a Housing Court case when he was caught at the metal detector. Court officers confiscated the fully loaded rifle magazine with 24 rounds, including a hollow-point bullet. Brown was charged with third degree criminal possession of a weapon and related crimes.

NEW YORK CITY: *Death, injury and chaos over no shoes?* A Brooklyn man killed his mother and stabbed his father during an argument over shoes, a police source reported in late-May 2019. Oscar Rodriguez Jr., 55, flew into a rage and plunged a knife into his mother, Maria, 77 when she tried to break up a fight between him and his father at their home. Rodriguez had returned home barefoot, and his father, Oscar, asked why he wasn't wearing his shoes. The son allegedly knifed his father in the arm and chest. Oscar Jr. was taken to a hospital psychiatric ward. His shoes were never found

WASHINGTON, D.C.: *The headline read, "Smoke gets in your eyes, and perhaps somewhere else.* An e-cig company has been marketing a new line of vape liquid purportedly containing Viagra and Cialis. However, a skeptical US food and Drug Administration issued a "stiff" warning to the firm to halt such sales.

MARYLAND: *The question was "SWATS" for dinner?* A supermarket shoplifter who was caught stealing hair accessories and a bag of chips thought she would escape store security by scaling the shelves and climbing into the ceiling of a Giant market in Baltimore. After ceiling tiles began to fall, the grocery store was forced to evacuate and call a SWAT team to extract the woman – who had taken merchandise worth $8.50. Nevertheless, they arrested her and sent her to jail.

MARYLAND: A Baltimore police officer has been found guilty of second-degree assault and misconduct in office after a video appeared to show him spitting on a man in handcuffs last year. Sgt. Robert Messner, a 34-year veteran, was sentenced recently to two years of probation, a $500 fine, anger management, community service, and reassignment.

RHODE ISLAND: *Police stop of driverless car.* Here is a first, a self-driving shuttle was pulled over by police on its first day carrying passengers on a new route. The Providence Police Chief said one of his officers pulled over the odd-looking vehicle because he had never seen one. The Chief said his officer stopped the vehicle because he had never seen one and he was curious. The officer said the vehicle looked like an oversize golf cart.

CHAPTER 2

A Bushel Basket Full of Pennsylvania Rogues

PENNSYLVANIA: *We'll bet liquor was somehow involved in this.* Pennsylvania police arrested a 57-year-old man, clad in just his underwear, when he jumped on the hood of his girlfriend's moving car during a quarrel in sub-freezing temperatures. Uniontown police had received a report at 3:20 am of a man sitting on the hood of a car yelling at the woman behind the wheel.

PENNSYLVANIA: *Take two of these and call your attorney in the morning.* A San Francisco man took a double dose of his medical marijuana cookies and freaked out aboard a US Airways jet in route from Philadelphia to LA, screaming, dropping his pants and fighting with the crew, and forcing the pilot to make an emergency landing in Pittsburgh. Kinman Chan, 30, was taken into FBI custody.

PENNSYLVANIA: *A real bone head...* The following story has to be dubbed a "do it yourself arrest." A man got drunk, stole a car, and drove to a state police barracks Wilkes-Barre, where he walked into the lobby and told troopers what he had done. He then also admitted that he had no driver's license.

PENNSYLVANIA: *Right...sick of having no booze!* A fugitive wanted for bank robbery in Michigan is in a Pennsylvania jail after he walked out of a Pittsburgh hospital and into a bar wearing only his hospital gown, with an IV needle still in his arm. Elbert Thompson, 20, walked four blocks from Allegheny General Hospital to Jr's Bar. Police found he was wanted in Michigan after a traffic stop. He had been hospitalized after saying he felt sick.

PENNSYLVANIA: *He took the name of the bar much too literally!* Police report that a man walked into a bar named "Shooters," in Wilkes-Barre, pulled a handgun and pumped a bullet into the toilet in the men's room. The toilet was destroyed. The report goes on to state that police "flushed" him out and arrested him soon after the shooting.

PENNSYLVANIA: *What a phone store...* Talk about customer service! A worker at a Philly-area mobile phone store has been accused of stabbing a customer who had come in the store to complain about being double billed. The customer survived the attack.

PENNSYLVANIA: *Perhaps he thought he was invisible....* A 300-pound man left security personnel at a Philly area Walmart dumbfounded when he walked into the store "buck-naked" and proceeded to shoplift a pair of socks. Police confronted him at the door and Tasered him when he ignored their command to stop.

PENNSYLVANIA: *We hope that he is not as fussy about jailhouse food.* Lyndel Topp, of Philly, was arrested after attacking his fiancé for making his meatball sandwich the "wrong" way. Topp became furious "due" to the fact that the victim not placing the cheese on his hoagie correctly," according to a police report. He allegedly grabbed a knife and nearly chopped off one of the woman's fingers before sinking his teeth into her wrist.

PENNSYLVANIA: *BAAAARRFFF.... Nasty buzzard!* A Philly man was sentenced in July 2014, to up to three months in jail for intentionally vomiting on another spectator and the spectator's 11-year-old daughter at a Phillies baseball game. Matthew Clemens, 21, of Cherry Hill, NJ, had pleaded guilty in May 2014 to charges of assault, harassment and disorderly conduct. Clemens admitted he stuck his finger down his throat and vomited on Michael Vangelo and his daughter. Clemens will be on probation for two years after he serves his jail sentence.

PENNSYLVANIA: *Boy, oh boy, nothin' like the luck of the Irish...* In Philly, a belt buckle saved a grocery worker by stopping a stray bullet that hit him from, a shootout outside. Bienvenido Reynoso, 38, who hit the ground after hearing shots didn't realize he was struck – until someone pointed out a hole in his shirt and he found the bullet in his belt buckle.

PENNSYLVANIA: *Drunk and dumb...bad combination!* A man allegedly assaulted a police officer who made a traffic stop of him for DUI on a lawn tractor. Mark Grove, 44, had a coffee mug full of beer sitting on his tractor. He allegedly told the office "I'm drunk. Just take me home." He then kicked the officer and, once in the police cruiser, head butted the protective partition between the front and back seat of the vehicle.

PENNSYLVANIA: *Those city officials are cretins...* A Philly city agency is threatening to sue a man if he doesn't return 40 tons of garbage to the weed strewn government lot that he deigned to clean up without the city's permission. Ori Felbush spruced up the trashy lot near his coffee shop, and the city is demanding he restore it to the condition in which he found it.

PENNSYLVANIA: *...And we thought justice was blind!* An assault trial in Philly came to a halt after the victim's prosthetic eye popped out as he testified about the attack that left him partially blind. While the man fished around for his $3,000 glass eye, the judge announced a recess due to the "unforeseen incident."

PENNSYLVANIA: *So, where is Robin Hood when you need him?* Kenneth Butterworth, a motorist in Philly, was upset about a driver who he believed had cut him off. So, he allegedly pulled out a medieval crossbow and pointed it at the other motorist. It is reported that no one was hurt. Butterworth had no arrows with him.

PENNSYLVANIA: *He had better go to confession straightaway.* A Roman Catholic priest was arrested for trying to buy cocaine in Philly. Police said they saw Father James Shimsky, 50, of the Diocese of Scranton, pull up to a dealer on the street and purchase a bag of coke. He has been ordered to take a leave of absence.

PENNSYLVANIA: *KA-BOOM ON THE BOOM BOOM!* This next one could be about an explosive bowel movement! Nikita Fulton is suing a Philadelphia company after she claimed its toilet blew up beneath her, causing severe back injuries. The woman said she was doing her business in a restroom when intense water pressure caused the ceramic bowl to burst and launched her into the ceiling.

PENNSYLVANIA: *What a poor escape artist!* James Williams, a Pittsburgh man was caught for allegedly driving a stolen car. When accosted by the police Williams jumped into the Ohio River before police nabbed him. At a hospital, Williams tried bolting again, by taking off his clothes and hiding in a dumpster. Again, he was caught shortly thereafter.

PENNSYLVANIA: *What a poor escape artist!* James Williams, a Pittsburgh man was caught for allegedly driving a stolen car. When accosted by the police Williams jumped into the Ohio River before police nabbed him. At a hospital, Williams tried bolting again, by taking off his clothes and hiding in a dumpster. Again, he was caught shortly thereafter.

CHAPTER 3

Florida Rogues on Parade

FLORIDA: *There's always room for one more….*
Florida sheriff deputies loading prisoners into a transport
van didn't have to work very hard to find one more
customer after a woman high on drugs side-swiped the
police van. Emily Spiess, 30, allegedly added injury to
insult when she ran over the foot of one of the deputies as
she was being arrested on assault and battery charges.

FLORIDA: *His luck ran out on him too soon.* A man
stole $10,000 worth of scratch-off lottery tickets in Ocala
Florida and tried to cash in one of the winners in
Leesburg, 30 miles away. The ticket came up void or
stolen at the Leesburg store, where the quick-witted clerk
snapped a photo of the man which helped police make his
arrest.

FLORIDA: *Pop, pop, pop...* A grand opening of a
restaurant erupted into an active shooter scare, after
customers mistook the sound of balloons popping for
bullets. Officials at a mall in Orlando, warned shoppers
about a balloon bursting stunt to celebrate the opening of
Joey Fatone's new restaurant, Fat One's. Still crowds
were panicked and ran for the doors, according to police
who rushed to the scene and found no guns.

FLORIDA: *Crystal meth donut frosting, maybe???* A Florida man is accusing police of wrongful arrest, claiming police arrested him after mistaking donut frosting for crystal meth. Dan Rushing, 64, of Orlando said he gave police permission to search his car after they stopped him for running through a stop sign. "They said, 'We found what we thought was crack cocaine in the beginning, but now think it's methamphetamine,'" he recalled. The meth turned out to be nothing more than Krispy Kreme. "Every Wednesday I stop at Krispy Kreme and get a donut there" he said. "And they found four little flakes of the icing." Court records reveal that Rushing was charged with possession of meth in the traffic stop. But the arrest was later voided a month later when the crime lab test showed it was, in fact icing. Police insist it was a lawful drug arrest because a roadside test showed the icing was meth. Rushing indicates that he is now considering a lawsuit. "I just don't want this to happen to anybody else," he said.

FLORIDA: *Vicious Swan? The headline read: "It was a fowl day for this police officer."* An unnamed police officer was caught on video fleeing from a swan that chased him out of Orlando's Lake Eola Park as he rode a bicycle. The Orlando Police Department tweeted the footage, noting, "You can't imagine the hazards our officers face out there every day."

FLORIDA: *As thin as an Auschwitz prisoner!* A woman was charged with neglect after the 96-year-old man she was supposed to be caring for showed up at a hospital so malnourished that he was just "skin and bones" and weighed only 89 pounds according to Apopka police. The man told police that his caretaker Alice K, 56, threatened to feed him dog feces and refused to let him eat. Police report that the doctor at the Florida Hospital Apopka likened him to an "Auschwitz prisoner." Police further reported that the man had been fed very little, if at all, over the last month. Upon being admitted the hospital called the Department of Children and families which then contacted the police. When he was fed at the hospital he started eating like a "starving dog," according to the treating doctor. Alice K was charged with neglect of an elderly person and was taken to the Orange County Jail and held on $500 bond. The elderly man remains in the hospital and will eventually be released to the care of DCF police said.

FLORIDA: *Spider man in a rainstorm?* We hear that neighbors were stunned when they spotted a man pressure-washing the roof of a home in Miramar – while dressed as Spider Man. A video shows Spidey blasting dirt away during a rainstorm. We do not know why…

FLORIDA: *The headline read: "Their mouths were clean, but their hands were dirty."* Orange County deputies allege that 64-year-old Mary Curtiss and 44-year-old Clint Curtis led a racketeering operation that was responsible for stealing more than $100,000 in electronic toothbrush products and cash from Publix, Walmart, Walgreens and CVS stories throughout central Florida. The criminal complaint further alleges that the bulk of the money the two brought in came from stealing two particularly unusual items—high-end electronic and replacement toothbrush heads – then returning them as if they had legitimately purchased and pocketing the cash. Not only were the corporations losing money in the stolen merchandise, but they also lost money each time their employees processed a return. The Curtiss's are being held in the Orange County Trial awaiting trial.

FLORIDA: *Wrong place, wrong time, wrong woman...* In this case a flasher pervert picked the wrong woman to expose himself to on a beach – a former federal law-enforcement agent. I was autumn in Florida and the retired federal officer was out for a stroll on Vero Beach near her home when 48-year-old Paris Lapointe allegedly took off his shorts and flashed his genitals. The victim called police and reported the perv who was arrested and charged with exposure of sexual organs.

FLORIDA: *The headline read: "Lady Lake police officer resigns after exposing himself." How sordid!* Officer Kevin Thompson resigned in early 2016 after allegations and photos surfaced of him masturbating in his patrol car in uniform for a Leesburg woman he met on Craigslist. The State Attorney's Office declined to file charges against the officer, but the police chief said the department's reputation has been tarnished. Officer Thompson, who is married, responded to the 38-year-old woman's Craigslist ad about four months prior to his resignation and the pair started meeting while he was on duty. He told investigators that his marriage was in disarray and he decided to look for companionship on the web. On the day of the incident it appears that outside of her workplace the woman walked up to Thompson's patrol car and saw that he had his pants down and was masturbating. She advised deputies he let her snap about 15 photos. Later, while trying to break off the affair she threatened to tell Thompson's wife about the affair and send her the photos. Thompson then threatened her for threatening a police officer.

FLORIDA: *"Cookie Monster alert," read the headline.* Police are hunting for a Sweet-toothed shoplifter who allegedly loaded his shopping cart to the brim with cookies and bolted from the store without paying. The bandit was seen in surveillance footage wheeling away the loot at a Miramar Family Dollar.

FLORIDA: *PETA protestor in killer whale garb arrested at the airport.* This odd story comes from Christmas Eve 2015, when a protester dressed as an Orca whale climbed atop a baggage carousel at Orlando International Airport and was arrested for trespassing. Bryan Wilson, 47, was one of two costumed people staging a demonstration on behalf of the people for the Ethical Treatment of Animals (PETA) during the busy holiday season. Wilson had refused to budge when asked by police. He was then arrested and removed in a wheelchair. Police report the arrest was to quell a hazardous public disturbance impacting airport operations. In a news release, PETA later maintained the protest was to dissuade tourists from visiting SeaWorld Orlando, where the organization contends the whales are forced to swim in "chemically treated water."

FLORIDA: *Con Man!!!* It has been reported that when attorney Kenneth Andrews first met his new client, Donald Mitchell, at the Seminole County jail, Mitchell walked out of lock up looking like a "superstar," while dressed in a white jail jumpsuit, not blue like most other inmates, and wearing tinted gold framed glasses. Mitchell was a star of sorts who gained cache while in the jail because he is the inmate who conned his lawyer into smuggling a new iPhone past corrections authority, an act that left the attorney locked up in the same jail. Mitchell also threatened a judge and tore up a jail security camera.

FLORIDA: *He typically mailed the letters. This time – bad news -- he showed up in person.* Orange County deputies say last Christmas, 2015, 69-year-old Jose Santana had sent 40 handwritten letters to his estranged wife of 45 years, threatening to hurt her and their family if she ever called the police. Nevertheless, she decided to call at Christmas when he hand-delivered the letter to her door. He left the letter at her door and departed. In the letter, deputies say that Santana wrote that "he wanted to decapitate her and make history in Florida." The letter further stated that "I want to hurt you so bad." and indicated further still that he was not afraid of going to jail. Records show that Santana's wife has filed for a domestic-violence injunction against him. He was arrested the day after Christmas on charges of stalking and making written threats to kill or do bodily harm.

FLORIDA: *Speedway burglar sent to the slammer.* A Georgia man convicted of burglarizing race-team trailers at Daytona International Speedway and other tracks was recently sentenced to prison. Prosecutors contend that 55-year-old Steven Sanders of Macon, Georgia was sentenced to ten years for the 13 burglaries at Daytona between 2007 and 2012. Court papers reveal that he would steal cash, credit cards and debit cards. He would also keep souvenirs from the thefts, including the racetrack credentials of actor Patrick Dempsey from televisions Grey's anatomy."

FLORIDA: *She had no sole.* A woman got so angry at a police officer for stopping her on the highway, she pulled off her shoes and threw them at his patrol car. Amber Capraro, 31, was walking in the middle of a highway in St. Lucie County when the officer tried to stop her. She allegedly flew into rage and threw her shoes at his car and jumped on the hood. Yes, she was arrested.

FLORIDA: *Unfortunately, sounds like gay sex-slave prostitution is alive and well in Florida!* A Hungarian man has been convicted in South Florida for his role in running what investigators called a gay sex-slave prostitution ring. Andras Janos Vass faces a minimum of 21 years and a maximum of 155 years in prison after a Miami jury convicted him in April 2015 of human trafficking and racketeering. Reported testimony from the trial revealed that Vass and others brought three victims to New York in 2012 and forced them to perform sex acts at all hours. The victims and their families in Hungary were threatened and the victims' travel documents were confiscated. The ring relocated to the Miami area later in 2012. We learn further that two other Hungarians are awaiting trial in the matter.

FLORIDA: *Nude basketballer?* A man who was shooting baskets in a public park naked received a foul called on him. Jordan Anderson, 29, was charged with indecent exposure for his play at Candyland Park in Longwood. Mr. Anderson told police he thought playing basketball in the buff would up his game, police said.

FLORIDA: *We wonder why he did not renew his concealed-carry license??* Late last year, 2015, a Miami man was arrested for carrying a handgun outside of Disney's Magic Kingdom. Andrew Gerson, a 36-year-old attorney actually faces charges of illegally carrying a concealed firearm. His concealed-carry license had expired a decade before in June of 2005. When a security guard checking bags at the entrance to the Magic Kingdom, she noticed a strange bulge in in his pants. When she asked what was in his pants, he said it was his anatomy. He then ran off. The security officer called an Orange County deputy who chased him and yelled for him to stop which he did. When the deputy asked whether he had a gun he said he did that he did and dropped to his knees. The handgun was confiscated. In addition to his arrest Gerson was given a "trespass," which prohibits him from returning to a Disney property. Disney World regulations forbid weapons being brought onto the property.

FLORIDA: *Seems she was the biggest demon.* We have learned that a self- proclaimed Florida psychic who charged an elderly woman more than $3.5 million for exorcisms and "spiritual cleansing" has pleaded guilty to tax evasion. Sally Johnson, 41, made this money between 2007 and 2014 by promising to rid the wealthy Massachusetts woman of demons

.

FLORIDA: *Bacon inside a mosque is never good! Vandalism at mosque called a Hate Crime.* We learn that an attack earlier this year at a mosque using raw bacon and a machete could perhaps draw a Brevard County man a sentence of up to life in prison as a result of a recently added hate-crime enhancement to Florida law. Michael Wolfe, 35, was charged with armed burglary of a structure and criminal mischief of a place of worship in connection with the New Year's Eve break-in and desecration of the Islamic Society of Central Florida Masjid Al-Munin Mosque in Titusville. An arrest report reveals that the convicted felon acted alone, broke into the empty mosque with a machete at night, slashing at windows and other property before leaving behind a slab of raw bacon in and around the front door. Wolfe's actions in the mosque were recorded on surveillance video. The State Attorney reviewed the case and brought formal charges on both counts which now carry hate-crime enhancements, which means the potential sanctions in the event of a conviction are increased. We learned that in the case of the armed burglary the enhancement could now draw a life sentence.

FLORIDA: *What a blockhead.* It has been reported that a Dunkin' donuts customer attempted to pay for coffee with prescription pain pills, according to police. Richard Bourque, 30, allegedly offered up the pills at a shop in Pinellas Park. When the cashier turned him down, he snatched the coffee and walked out without paying. We learn that the man was later arrested.

FLORIDA: *How utterly stupid! They called this one a "rip off tip off!"* A thief stole two men's wallets only to drop his own in an awkward getaway attempt. Levoris Pace, 28, allegedly pulled a handgun and demanded two pals sitting in a car to hand over their money in Panama City, according to a police report. Pace ran off with $600 in cash but police found his wallet near the scene of the heist, leading to Pace's request.

FLORIDA: *Free samples or spree samples??* A 20-year-old Florida woman was arrested after she sped around a Walmart in a motorized shopping cart, munching on rotisserie chicken, sushi, cinnamon rolls, and downing it all with a bottle of wine. Josseleen Lopez allegedly consumed $32.36 worth of food and beverage from the store. Of course, she was arrested on a shoplifting "beef," yuk, yuk...

FLORIDA: *Assault with a deadly weapon: baby??* Police report that during the Fourth of July weekend 2016, an 18-year-old mother was charged with using her infant son as a deadly weapon to bludgeon her boyfriend at Daytona Beach. Daytona Beach police arrested Tatyana Allen of Ocoee, Florida for swinging the baby "like a bat" during a fight at the beach. The police report indicates that the 6-month-old baby boy was taken to a local hospital where it appeared that he was doing fine.

FLORIDA: *Psycho?* Recently a man was found naked, spouting gibberish while standing in a fire in his front yard. John Hennessey, 37, of Cape Coral, allegedly greeted police who tried to rescue him by waving a knife, and then a stick at them. Hennessey, believed to be high on psychedelic mushrooms, was arrested and charged with assault and criminal mischief.

FLORIDA: *Good Samaritans, maybe?* A man re-sodding his lawn suddenly had a heart attack. As he was put in an ambulance, he worried out loud to the EMT medics about expecting a fine from his neighborhood association if the lawn job was not completed on time. So, after leaving the man at the hospital seven of his rescuers sped back to his house and finished the work.

FLORIDA: *Fall guy or fall dog?* A motorist arrested for allegedly driving while impaired told police his dog was behind the wheel. Scott Garrett, 56, was driving his 2005 Nissan near Port St. Lucie when an officer pulled him over for swerving and found an open bottle of spiced rum, said police. However, Garrett continued to maintain that his dog was doing the driving. His dog was not charged – but he was.

FLORIDA: *Bad excuse...* A driver told police his behind the wheel drinking didn't amount to DWI – because he only downed swigs of whiskey at stop signs. Police didn't agree with him. Earle Stevens, 69, was allegedly drunk when his car tapped a woman's car at a Vero Beach McDonald's drive thru. Police found a bottle of Jim Beam beside him in his car.

FLORIDA: *"Yo quiero English lessons," read the headline*. Taco Bell recently fired a South Florida employee for refusing to take an order from a customer who did not speak Spanish according to the Miami Herald. "This is Hialeah!" the worker reportedly retorted in Spanish, apparently referring to the city's large Spanish-speaking population.

FLORIDA: *First Amendment Idiot?* Dillon Webb, 33, is defending what he calls his First Amendment right to a bumper sticker that proclaims his sexual appetites. However, authorities in Lake City have charged Mr. Webb of violating obscenity laws and resisting an order to remove the sticker form his car which treads: "I eat ass."

FLORIDA: *They call it "buff luck."* We learn that South Florida residents have complained about neighbors doing outdoor chores in the nude. Residents in the town of Stuart complained about their neighbors gardening, putting out trash, and working on his car without clothes. The Martin County Sheriff's Department told them they can't do anything about the display of privates on private property. In other words – buff luck.

CHAPTER 4

A Bunch of Rogues from the Old South

ALABAMA: *Happy July Fourth!* A car dealer has rolled out a new Fourth of July promotion for summer 2019, which offers a Bible, a 12-gauge shotgun, and an American flag with every car purchase. "I just want to reach out to everybody in the area and let y'all know we will be celebrating the Fourth a little bit different this year," Coby Palmer of Chatom Ford in Chatom says in a video that has gone viral.

ALABAMA: *They say he gave up the cloth, literally.* A minister had a big career change when he became a gay porn actor at 83. Norm Self, now 85, joined the clergy at 18 and came out as gay in 1997. We learn he did is first scene pro-bono in 2017 and calls his new calling "almost like having a party."

ALABAMA: *Big, big fright!* It has been reported that an intruder wearing nothing but a Ronald Reagan mask and sock covering his genitals gave an Alabama couple quite a fright. Bart Yancey saw the skulking man in his front hallway when he went to take out the garbage. Upon seeing Yancey, the masked intruder ran off without taking anything or hurting anyone.

ALABAMA: *Goldilocks in Bama?* It has been reported that a man allegedly broke into a house, made himself breakfast, took a bath and washed his clothes. Mary Royster said she came home on a Tuesday in mid-October and found a strange man who wouldn't leave – he told her he was waiting for his clothes to dry. He had also gone through her drawers, made scrambled eggs, shaved and brushed his teeth. Tyler Love, 31, is now back at the Limestone County Jail on a charge of burglary. He had been released the week before after serving time for an earlier burglary.

ARKANSAS: *Udder disregard for the law?* It has been reported that Ashley Curry, 27, was dressed in a cow costume when she told police to "suck a pink cow udder" after they had detained her on suspicion of shoplifting. She had tried to steal a package of Flonase nasal spray from a Pine bluff Walmart, police report.

GEORGIA: *Someone let go of their Legos too soon.* A 3-year-old got a surprise when he opened a box of Legos and found nothing but a large haul of meth inside. The tot's relatives bought the toy plastic blocks at a consignment shop in Charleston and brought it home to Statesboro. The box was shrink-rapped to appear new and came complete with more than three pounds of meth with a street value of $40,000.

GEORGIA: *Hello 911…* Georgia police recently issued an arrest warrant for William Baccus, 62, who called police more than 100 times over the past three years – to ask them to bring him milk, his cell phone, a TV remote control, and many other silly non-emergency requests, Cobb County police said. Mr. Baccus faces a charge of abuse of the 911 emergency system.

GEORGIA: *The questions is – "Where did he put the cocktail sauce?"* A man allegedly purloined a bag of frozen shrimp by shoving it down the front of his pants. Unfortunately, his pants gave off a distinctive crunching sound as he was leaving the Dollar General store in Albany. The man was confronted by the store manager but managed to leave with his purloined seafood.

KENTUCKY: *Possible courtroom drug dealing?* A Mount Olive woman allegedly arrested for making terroristic threats tried to sell meth inside a courtroom while she waited for the judge to take the bench. A security guard said he overheard Telby Fields, 24, trying to hawk the drug to three people in the back of the courtroom. Ms. Fields alleged bolted from the courtroom and led police on a chase that ended with her arrest.

LOUISIANA: *He got the 411 the hard way…* It has been reported that Christian Palacios, 24, called police in the town of Thibodaux to learn whether he had any active warrants out for his arrest. Police confirmed that he had no warrants but charged him with unlawful use of 911 to make a non-emergency call.

LOUSIANA: *No sex, no peace?* A woman opened fire on a man after he denied her oral sex, according to a police report. Anneisha Speed, 19, allegedly warned the man, with whom she had been "hanging out" all day in Baton Rouge, that she would shoot him if he didn't perform oral sex on her. He didn't – so she fired row shots at him with a .40-caliber handgun, police said. The man managed to escape with no injuries. We do not learn whether an arrest was made.

MISSISSPPI: *"Pol's punch-drunk sex arrest," read the headline.* We learn that a state lawmaker punched his wife in the face and bloodied her nose after she didn't undress quickly enough when he wanted to have sex, according to police. republican state Rep. Doug McLeod of Lucedale was arrested on a misdemeanor charge of domestic violence in mid-May 2019.

NORTH CAROLINA: *So stupid!* A woman kept her mother's body at home for several months to satisfy her curiosity about the "stages of death." Police said. When Donna Sue Hudgins, 69, of the town of Enfield, eventually went to a funeral home to make arrangements for her mother, Nellie May Hudgins, 93, Donna was arrested and charged with concealment of a death.

NORTH CAROLINA: *Sounds like James also Got Fingered.* A father was pulled over for a broken taillight while driving his daughter to school, and it turned out he had an open arrest warrant. For what? He had an open arrest warrant for failing to return a VHS tape of "Freddy Got Fingered" in 2002. Fourteen years' worth of late fees caused James Meyers to land in the pokey. Shortly after he was pulled over by police in the town of Concord deputies advised Meyers that in North Carolina not returning rental property is a misdemeanor and punishable by a fine up to $200. Meyers was allowed to take his daughter to school, as long as he promised to turn himself in the same day.

VIRGINIA: *The right shoe?* We learn that two thieves swiped specialty sneakers from a shop in Roanoke – only to learn the shoes were all made for the right foot. The bandits broke into Clean Soles and made off with 13 shoes, police report. However, owner Rob Wickham said he keeps only the right shoes on display and the left ones stashed behind the counter. Thieves will have a hard time on the run.

VIRGINIA: *Did the supermarket throw out the produce?* In mid-September 2018 a man was arrested for "rubbing produce on his bare buttocks at a supermarket and reshelving it, according to police. Dwayne Johnson, 27, allegedly strolled into a Giant food store in Manassas, pulled down his pants and went to town on the fruits, said police. He was charged with indecent exposure and destruction of property.

WEST VIRGINIA: *"Tanks for nothing,"* read the *headline*. Residents blamed a disrespectful prank when a vintage tank on display in a local park was painted neon yellow and lime green. As it turns out, that a club at Bluefield State College that maintains the tank accidentally ordered the wrong colors, instead of the usual olive green. No disrespect intended.

TENNESSEE: *"Kiddie Hitlers' nixed,"* read the *headline*. An elementary school in Rutherford County will no longer have a student portray Adolf Hitler in its living-history exhibit after a group of children began giving Nazi salutes. A school district spokesman said that the boy portraying Hitler was supposed to give a speech and a Nazi salute, but other students then started giving the salute in an out of rehearsals. The spokesman also said that the school district does not condone "hate-filled or insensitive" action symbols.

TENNESSEE: *A very controversial theme park, indeed?* It has been reported that a theme park hawking a virtual-reality ride that recreates the crash that killed Princess Diana is set to open in the last week of May 2019 in the town of Pigeon Forge. The National Enquirer Live! Park charges $25 for the attraction, which features a computer-generated scene of the August 1997 paparazzi chase in Paris.

TENNESSEE: *Flighty Booze Bust?* We learn that a Delta Air Lines flight attendant has been charged with stealing 1,500 mini-bottles of liquor from her job and selling them online. Rachel Trevor, 28, has been indicted on charges including theft, unlawful sale of alcohol and unauthorized transportation of alcohol, according to the Shelby County District Attorney's office. The indictment alleges that she would put small bottles in her bag after a flight, and then post them for sale on Craigslist. The bottles sell for $8 on flights, but Ms. Trevor was allegedly selling them for $1 apiece.

CHAPTER 5

A Few Mid-West Rogues

ILLINOIS: *Meth-soaked coloring book?* A jailed idiot asked his girlfriend to ship him a meth-soaked coloring book so he could sell pages of it behind bars, authorities said. Daniel McClure, 36, an inmate at the Macon County Jail, allegedly sold more than $2,800 worth of the speed-laced art, which users chewed to get high. McClure was done in by drug-sniffing dogs and charged with drug conspiracy and delivery.

ILLINOIS: *Not the real boss?* It was reported in September of 2018, a Chicago woman who goes by the name of Mary was scammed out of $11,500 by a Bruce Springsteen impersonator she met online. For more than a year, Mary swapped messages with the phony via a fake Facebook page before he asked for money and she sent it. "It hurts, and you feel so stupid," she said.

KANSAS: *Nope, he didn't learn his lesson.* An accused car thief was released from jail – only to immediately steal another vehicle from the jailhouse parking lot, according to police. Security footage shows Kevin Jones, 33, stealing the car right outside the Shawnee County Jail in Topeka. He was sent right back to the same pokey.

MICHIGAN: *The headline read, "She's hell on wheels."* A Detroit woman in a wheelchair fired a Taser at a McDonald 's employee for not moving fast enough. The woman became impatient after placing her order and then fired the stun gun at the worker – but missed. Police took the Taser, but she was not immediately charged with a crime.

MICHIGAN: *Some say he is now in the doghouse.* It has been reported that a man put his two German shepherds in a car wash because they were covered with feces. As a result, dog lovers are "barking mad." Marshall Bullard blasted the dogs with scalding hot water from a high-pressure hose at Wash Stop Auto Wash in the town of Warren, outraging animal-rights advocates. Bullard said he rescued the filthy dogs from a neglectful owner earlier in the day. The dogs were taken to a vet and were pronounced unharmed.

MICHIGAN: *NO!* We learn that an 11-year-old boy scared away a home invader raiding the family fridge. Young Nathan Markos, of Battle Creek, was watching TV when he heard a noise in the kitchen and confronted the refrigerator bandit. When the brazen bandit asked if it was OK to take some drinks, the boy yelled NO, and the thief bolted out of the back door.

MINNESOTA: *"Now she's in hot water,"* read the *headline*. A grandmother got so mad at her grandson for placing a cup of tea on her precious wooden table, she shot him in the leg, according to police. Helen Washington, 75, of Brooklyn Center, allegedly dumped out the tea, then fetched her .38 special and fired one round into the thigh of her unidentified grandson. Yes, she was arrested.

MISSOURI: *Large A-hole?* Someone in Kansas City stole a large inflatable colon used to teach about the dangers of colon cancer. The 10-foot-long 150-pound inflatable with a value of $44,000 is owned by the Cancer Coalition, which hosts walking and running events under a campaign with the slogan "Get Your Rear in Gear."

MISSOURI: *Consensual Rape?* It has been reported that a state legislator is under fire for using the term "consensual rape" while defending an abortion-ban proposal. "Most of them were date rapes or consensual rapes," Rep Barry Hovis said in 2019 about the sexual assaults he handled during his time as a police officer. Rep. Raychel Proudie fired back, "There is no such thing – no such thing as consensual rape." Hovis later apologized.

MISSOURI: *The headline read, "The bull fought the law and the law won!"* Yet, that is not the whole story. We learn that police were called to keep a bull out of traffic and corral it after it escaped from a vet's clinic in the town of Mexico. Mission accomplished but only after the bull ran into a police cruiser, doing minor damage. Yep, the bull fought the law and the law won – but not before the bull left its mark on the police car.

OHIO: *This fellow needed obedience training, not his dog.* The man whose name was not released, flipped out at a TSA checkpoint at Cleveland Hopkins Airport and bit a police officer in early May 2019. Police took the man to a hospital for a psych exam and his dog was sent to a city-owned kennel.

OHIO: *Her bacon could be headed to jail, read the headline.* A grocery worker admittedly stole $9,200 worth of ham and salami – by eating about four slices a day for eight years on the job. A tipster alerted a loss prevention officer at the Giant Eagle supermarket in the town of Bolivar to the eater cheater. The hungry "Hamburglar" admitted to stealing the bites, and police are weighing whether to charge her.

OKLAHOMA: *Bacon flavored Bloody Mary Mix bust?* A bartender was arrested for infusing vodka with bacon – infuriating his boss, who alleges that he will take the police to court over this. Police contend that soaking the meat in alcohol violates state liquor-production laws. However, the bar owner stands by his special Bloody Mary blend.

OKLAHOMA: *A suspicious drone in OK bites the dust!* It has been reported that a legal drone used by a construction company to inspect gutters on a home in Edmond, was shot down by a frightened woman who lived nearby. "Somebody thought… they were spying so the neighbor came out and shot it down," said a spokesman for the County Sheriff's Office.

WISCONSIN: *Church "High" Holy days.* We learn that a Rastafarian house of worship in Madison, is distributing marijuana as a "sacrament." The Lion of Judah House of Rastafari Church's co-founder Jesse Schworck said he is giving away the devil's lettuce, claiming he is shielded by religious protections in the Bill of Rights

WISCONSIN: *Strange Names?* We learn that a woman named Marijuana Pepsi Vandyck earned her doctorate degree at with a dissertation on what else? – strange names. The Cardinal Stritch University student's writing centered on how African Americans with unusual names are treated in academia. Ms. Vandyck assures us that she doesn't partake in pot and does not drink soda. So, there.

WISCONSIN: *Mosquito crime fighters?* A bandit led police on a high- speed chase, then decided to abandon his car and hid out in a cornfield. – only to be foiled by a swarm of mosquitoes. The unidentified man allegedly had stolen liquor from a Piggly Wiggly market in the town of Campbellsport, before making a break for it. Bites from the mosquitoes got so bad, he surrendered to police.

CHAPTER 6

Rogues from Texas & the West

TEXAS: *Rogue Reptile?* A Walmart worker found a large-scale surprise at the bottom of a shopping cart-4-foot-long rat snake. The employee was gathering grocery carts outside the store in the town of Crossroads when a police officer heard a loud scream and rushed to help. The rogue reptile was wrangled and relocated by a "snake charmer," police said.

TEXAS: *At least he did not have "Gin & Juice" with Snoop.* A state trooper has been reprimanded for posing for a photo with Snoop Dogg at the South by southwest festival in Austin because the rapper has several convictions for drug possession. Billy Spears was working security at the March 2015 event when Snoop Dogg asked to take a picture with him. The artist posted the image on his social media. Spears came under investigation when his office learned of the photo. Spear's lawyer argued that his client did not know about the rapper's criminal record. However, Spears can't appeal the citation because it isn't a formal disciplinary action.

TEXAS: *Girl snatching...* Michael Webb, 51, was arrested and charged in the abduction of an 8-year-old girl who had been snatched from a street in Fort Worth as she walked with her mother one Saturday in May 2019. Police report the girl was found safe eight hours later at a nearby hotel. Web had grabbed the little girl and sped away with her in his car, according to the girl's mother. Police found Webb and the child after a witness reported seeing the car at a hotel. The girl was not harmed, and Webb was charged with aggravated kidnapping.

TEXAS: *UGH!* We learn that a San Antonio police officer accused of trying to feed a homeless man a dog-feces sandwich will not lose his job over the act, but he is still suspended for another "poop" related incident. An appeal panel tossed out the sandwich case because of the statute of limitations. Nevertheless, Matthew Luckhurst is still deep in it for more recently allegedly smearing a brown substance on a lady's restroom toilet seat.

ARIZONA: *Burrito Smuggling – some snack, huh?* A woman was arrested for smuggling a burrito stuffed with a pound of crystal meth over the Arizona border from Mexico. Customs authorities discovered that Susy Laborin's Mexican food had an extra kick to it after drug-sniffing dogs targeted her bag. The bag allegedly contained two burritos, one of which held the "speed." The meth was valued by Customs agents at $3,000.

COLORADO: *Nuns on the run!!* A man hopped a fence and for some reason chased a little old nun around a convent. The nun-chaser was but one of three rogues who have jumped over the six-foot fence at the Littleton Carmelite Order of Discalced Carmelite in the past year. We learn that the nuns have since asked the city for permission to build an eight-foot-high fence. *Good luck!*

COLORADO: *"FAKE!"* We learn that recently would-be marijuana thieves in Colorado Springs fell for the oldest trick in the book – mistaking oregano for marijuana. Four teenage bandits allegedly broke into Native Roots, a weed shop, by smashing a van through the glass entrance. They then made off with a stash of pre-rolled "joints" from a glass case. However, owner Kim Casey said she used a culinary herb to "simulate' the real thing in the display.

WYOMING: *A whiff of scandal...* A city council candidate is not dropping out despite a possible scandal. Deborah Reno, an Evanston yoga instructor and massage therapist, confirmed reports, confirmed reports that she spent the last year moonlighting as Mystee Crockett, selling Web-cam stripteases and used panties. 'That does not make me a weak or bad person," she wrote online. "It is a small, tiny part of who I am.

CHAPTER 7

Rogues of California & the Pacific Coast

CALIFORNIA: *The headline read, "Dog sitter more shag than wag."* We learn that a woman hired a pet sitter through the dog-walking app Wag and spotted the person naked in her home when she checked the puppy cam. Turns out that Rosie Brown booked 26-year-old pet sitter Casey Brengle to take care of her two pups, but instead the woman invited her boyfriend to the home for a romp in Ms. Brown's bed. In her defense Ms. Brengle claimed "It got hot and she doesn't like wearing clothes.

CALIFONIA: *To catch a predator?* A college student used Snapchat's gender-swap filter to pose as a 16-year-old girl on Tinder – and caught a 40-year-old police officer trying to meet the teen for sex. We assume the officer lost his job.

CALIFORNIA: *Wedding Crasher....?* Denise Gunderson, 50, was arrested for posing as a guest at several San Diego weddings and helping herself to the swag bags of the guests, brides and bridal party. She pleaded guilty to grand theft and identity theft and was sentenced to seven years in prison.

CALIFORNIA: *Flaming Poo, maybe?* Vandals lit portable toilets on fire at San Francisco's China Basin Beach, causing a big flaming mess. "It was a pretty big fire. Flames were lighting up the place," a nearby neighbor said. Fortunately, no one was injured but the vandals caused $30,000 in damage to the beach, which had to be temporarily closed.

CALIFORNIA: Pooey Puiton? We learn that the fashion brand Louis Vuitton sued the makers of a poo-emoji shaped handbag named "Pooey Puiton" – but their legal argument "stinks" said a LA judge who tossed out the suit.

CALIFORNIA: *Bong shaped AR-15 rifle leads to an arrest?* Police in San Diego swarmed a building on a Tuesday in early May 2019, when a man appeared to have waved what looked like an assault rifle out of a window. Concerned witnesses said they, "had seen a man pointing what looked to be a rifle from a window. Officers on patrol set up a perimeter around the area and went up to the room to question and detain Justin Baxley, 22. Once inside police found the gun-shaped glass bong, police said. The pot-smoking device had a realistic hand grip similar to an AR-15 rifle. Mr. Baxley was charged with exhibiting a replica firearm in a threatening manner, authorities said.

CALIFORNIA: *Low speed-chase?* The police report that a "hillbilly" was arrested when he led police on a "very low speed-chase -- on his tractor. When officers tried to pull over the man for driving erratically in Rancho Cordova, he hit the gas. However, during the 20-minute chase the bumpkin made it only one mile.

CALIFORNIA: *Why a potato?* It has been reported that a man has been convicted of burglary for breaking into a house and threatening to hit a woman with a potato that had her first initial carved into it. Police collared William Best, 41, in mid-September 2108. Best told police he used the potato to "increase his punching power.

CALIFORNIA: *The headline read, simply, "Freeze"* Two Long Beach drug dealers were arrested for selling marijuana and meth from their ice cream truck, police said. The truck, plastered images of ice cream sandwiches and popsicles was only a front, said police – who tossed suspects Monti Ware,41 and George Williams 57, in the cooler.

HAWAII: *Aztec calendars, NOT!* A group of eight suspected drug traffickers tried to be artful dodgers, allegedly disguising large amounts of methamphetamine as decorative Aztec calendars and statues in shipments to Hawaii. The dope was part of a nearly 90-poud shipment of ornamental replicas of 500-year-old Aztec calendar stone, authorities said.

OREGON: It appears that feathers were flying at the tax collector's office. Louis Adler, 66, was so angry with the tax department that he brought seven live chickens with him to the Eugene Office of the Oregon Department of Revenue. Adler was cited for trespassing and banned from the building. The chickens were taken to an animal shelter, however not before they relieved themselves in the Revenue office.

OREGON: *These burglars actually picked someone else's nose.* That's right burglars stole a 50-pound, 2-foot-tall plastic nose that was a Portland's family's beloved porch ornament. The discarded prop from an ad agency shoot was swiped on a Sunday in mid-October 2018, according to owner Delia Albert, who said, "We had a lot of good laughs with the nose."

WASHINGTON: *"Look up in the sky, is it a bird? Is it a plane? No, it's a penis, read the headline."* The Navy Times has revealed – two years after the fact – that the skywriting phallus that suddenly appeared above the state was created by two bored Navy pilots. "Draw a giant penis, that would be awesome," one of them said. "I could definitely draw one," the other replied, saying he would use the plane's exhaust. The cockpit hijinks got both pilots disciplined.

CHAPTER 8

We End With Rogues from Abroad

AUSTRALIA: *Caught for burglary on cameras they stole?* It appears that a group of bumbling thieves were accidently recording themselves committing a burglary and getting high afterward. "Surveillance cameras were stolen during the incident – all the while live-streaming footage of the burglary was being sent to the owner's mobile phone," Queensland police said.

AUSTRALIA: *"He put the speed near the crack,"* *read the headline.* A drug smuggler was arrested with nearly $1 million in crystal meth stuffed in his underwear, at an airport, police said. The 32-year-old man had just flown from Sydney to Hobart when police dogs sniffed out the junk in his trunk that weighed more than two pounds, according to drug authorities.

AUSTRALIA: *On the Run, literally.* A prisoner escaped from a prison van at a convenience store aptly named "On the Run." Shane Gauci, 41, asked to use the bathroom, then suddenly bolted at around 8:30 am on a Monday in late September 2018, in Adelaide, according to authorities. Gauci, who had been participating in a community program, is said to be still on the run.

AUSTRALIA: *Headline: "Wife crashes her own funeral – husband horrified that she was alive!"* What a story. Early in 2016, Mrs. Noela Rukundo sat in a car outside of her home in Melbourne, watching as the last few mourners filed out. They were leaving a funeral. As a matter of fact, it was her funeral. Finally, she saw the man for whom she had been waiting. She stepped out of her car and her husband put his hands on his head in horror. Why? It was just five days earlier that he had ordered a team of hit men to kill Rukundo, his wife of ten years. The hit met told her husband that they had killed her, but they never carried out the crime. The hit men had taken the money but said that they did not kill women. Her husband wailed, "I am sorry for everything." Too late, Rukundo had called the police and her husband, Balenga Kalala, ultimately pleaded guilty and was sentenced to nine years in prison for incitement to murder. What a story…

AUSTRALIA: *No FWD – no frying while driving*! Police in the city of Adelaide, spotted a strange-looking Mazda and pulled it over to find its steering wheel had been replaced with a frying pan. Police impounded the car after they discovered that the 32-year-old driver was uninsured.

AUSTRAILIA: *Some mix up or was it "some Meth up."* A senior couple in Melbourne, mistakenly signed for a package sent to the wrong address, and it contained 44 pounds of methylamphetamine – worth $10 million. The pair called the police who tracked down and arrested the alleged sender, Zhiling Ma, 21, of Melbourne.

AUSTRALIA: *The headline read: "He robbed himself blind."* A clumsy bandito accidently pepper-sprayed himself, according to a police report. The thief and a partner stole sleep-apnea gear and ran from a Perth pharmacy, but a worker chased them down. One of the bandits whipped out a can of Mace. Unfortunately, the can was facing the wrong direction when he pressed down on the nozzle.

BRAZIL: *Ha, ha – some joke…* A man was arrested for trying to extinguish the Olympic torch by throwing a bucket of water over it as it passed through the farming town of Maracaju in Brazil in late June 2016. Police arrested the 27-year-old-man at the scene for damaging public property. A video of the incident showed that the Olympic flame continued to burn. The unidentified man faces a 6 month to a three-year prison sentence for his stunt. The man said he tried to extinguish the flame as a joke.

BURKINA FASO: *Just how big were their Bim Bims?* We learn that this western African nation recently banned an annual beauty contest for women with the biggest rear-ends. The last weekend in August of 2016, would have been the third annual *Miss Bim Bim* pageant before government officials cancelled it for being too sexist and degrading. "Our role is to do everything to avoid damaging the image of our women," said Minister Laure Zongo.

CANADA: *Blatant Discrimination!!! All dolls matter...* Some shoppers in Canada are mad at a toy shop that charges more for white dolls than black ones. The Toys R Us in Calgary charged $24.99 for white you & Me Kissing Baby Doll and only $22.99 for the same doll with darker skin, angry parents said.

CANADA: *Waitress says her boss is a boob for forcing her to wear a bra on the job.* Christiana Schell, of British Columbia, is suing the Osoyoos Golf Club, allegeding she was fired for refusing to comply with the "sexist" dress code. Women working at the club's restaurant are required to wear a tank top or bra under their uniform, which she called a "human rights violation."

CANADA: *Could this summer vacation been a crime?* A Canadian teen called 911 in August of 2016 to report that her parents had "forced" her to go on vacation with them to Ontario. Police determined that there was no real emergency involved and cited the 15-year-old for improper use of the 911 system.

CANADA: *PHEW!* It has been reported that residents in an Ottawa neighborhood went without mail for more than a week because carriers refused to deliver to homes on a route where a skunk had been roaming. When a resident asked the post office about it officials put the blame on the bushy-tailed stinker.

CANADA: *Abuse of the Mails?* A woman was arrested for trying to send two puppies and a kitten through the mail. Jill Marshall 53, of Alberta was charged with causing animals to be in distress after she crammed them in boxes with postage on the outside and stamps on their heads.

CANADA: *Burglar cleaners?* Two women were arrested for breaking into a house in Nova Scotia – to clean it, according to police. The homeowner called police to report the intruders had entered through an unlocked door and had gone to work with a mop and a vacuum. It turned out the women, who were professional cleaners, had gone to the wrong address. No arrests were made.

COLOMBIA: *Holy cow, Holy water?* A Catholic priest is on a mission to exorcise the demons from the city of Buenaventura, by dumping holy water on the city from an airplane. Monsignor Ruben Dario Montoya says the town has gone to hell with a shocking 51 murders in five months. He has been working with the country's navy and the city's mayor to get a plane for the mid-July 2019 cleansing.

COLOMBIA: *Cheater?* An angry Uber driver caught his wife having an affair when she and her lover unwittingly hired him to drive them to a Barranquilla hotel. The husband, identified by police as Yeimy, brawled with the lover when he showed up in a friend's car his wife hadn't recognized.

CHINA: *They term it China's "forbidden fruit."* It has been reported that officials have banned videos in China of attractive people eating bananas. Web firms have been forced to crack down on users, often beautiful women, who stream videos of themselves chowing down on what is considered the "phallic fruit." Government officials started cracking down on such videos in May 2016, declaring a war against "inappropriate and erotic" web content.

CHINA: *The headline read – Knock it off!* We learn that shops in Hong Kong are being discouraged from selling knock-off paper versions of clothes to burn as part of a Chinese tradition. Authorities at the Gucci Corporation learned of the shops selling paper versions of their clothes to burn as offering to the deceased and demanded shop owners stop selling the counterfeit clothes.

CHINA: *A Chinese driver reached for the stars and got his car towed.* The young motorist, who has 27 tickets on his record, offered a tale from outer space when he was pulled over in Zhejiang province. "You have your regulations, but we have our regulations in the Milky Way as well. I'm from a royal family. If you let me go, then I will let this incident pass. But, if you piss me off, I will be forced to destroy the Earth," he raved in a caught-on camera rant. His car was then towed to an impound lot.

DENMARK: *Pervert alert!!* A flasher on roller skates is on the loose in Denmark, where he has shocked at least three women in parks. The roller pervert usually hides in bushes in Tjaereborg before exposing himself – and then rocketing away on his getaway skates. No arrest has been made but police are hunting for the man described as being in his 20's and has dark hair.

FRANCE: *A government handout that is a real turn-on?* It has been reported that the Mayor of Montereau, a 650-person French town near Paris, is giving away free Viagra to couples to encourage them to make babies. "A village without children is a village that dies," said Mayor Jean Debouzy.

FRANCE: *Things don't always go better with coke, stupid!* A woman was so curious about the quality of her cocaine that she walked into a police station and asked gendarmes to test it. The 43-year-old asked police in Toulouse to examine two bags of cocaine and one bag of crack "because she wanted to know if it was good quality," said police. Of course, she was arrested and sent to jail.

GERMANY: *Sex at the top of the bridge!* A German couple who took exhibitionism to new heights were arrested for indulging in sexual intercourse on top of a bridge. It appears that the lovers climbed hundreds of feet onto an arch of the Kaiserlei Bridge in Frankfurt, peeled of their clothes and proceeded to do the "wild thing." Police had to close the Autobahn to bring the couple down and arrest them for lewd public behavior.

GERMANY: *Kliene Dumkopf (Little Dummy)*. A young boy pulled off a great heist when he stole a bus – and none of the passengers even noticed the lad was behind the wheel. The 11-year-old troublemaker said he found a key to the privately-owned bus and decided to take it for a joyride in Ingolstadt. No one was injured and the boy was released to his mother.

GERMANY: *OOOPPPPSSS!!* It has been reported that a little old lady filled out a crossword puzzle at a German museum only to find it was piece of modern art worth $89,000. The 1965 artwork by artist Arthur Koepcke featured the phrase "insert words" which the 91-year-old woman took too literally. Official at Nuremberg's Neues Museum called police but the owner just laughed it off, insisting that that the piece could be restored.

GERMANY: *Nude awakening?* They say police were in for a "nude" awakening when they stopped a naked man riding a motorbike during a recent heat wave. Brandenburg police said they gave a warning to the man, that he needed to wear more than just his helmet and sandals. Their tweet with him went viral.

HUNGARY: *Pig heads??* A Hungarian member of the European parliament whipped up controversy in mid-August 2016 by suggesting that displaying pig heads on a border fence would be an effective way to scare Muslim immigrants from entering the EU-member country. Gyorgy Schopflin made the suggestion in response to local putting u carved root-vegetable, human-like masks at the border.

INDIA: *The headline read, "Someone is in hot water."* A $3 billion Indian naval submarine sank because an idiot forgot to close one single hatch. The vessel, dubbed the INS Arihant, is out of commission after water flooded its propulsion compartment, causing major damage.

INDIA: *Dead cell phone – dead beat passenger?* It has been reported that a drunken passenger was recently thrown off an IndiGo plane at Mumbai's airport after he tried to enter the cockpit while the airplane was still on the ground. His reason? He wanted to charge his cellphone. Idiot...

INDIA: *"Give him a reward – or else..."* We learn that a servant who saved his boss from being knifed was so angry that his employer skimped on a thank you gift, he stole $96,000 from him. Dhan Singh Bisht, 37, of Delhi, fought off bandits who threatened to cut his boss' throat in August 2018, authorities report. When his employer "rewarded" him with just a T-shirt, he allegedly hatched a plan to steal. Unfortunately, Bisht was arrested and sent to jail.

KUWAIT: *A case of shady fishmongers...* It has been reported that a seafood store was shut down after it was arrested for sticking googly eyes on fish to make them appear fresher. Photos show the craft supplies poorly masking the glassy eyes of one long dead creature.

IRELAND: *Great-grandfather thrashes criminal thugs*. It has been reported that this senior citizen fought off three weapon-wielding robbers with his bare hands. The bad boys were hauling hammers and a sawed-off shotgun when they stormed 83-year-old Dennis O'Conner's sports betting center Bar One Racing in Glanmire and demanded cash. Instead of backing down, O'Conner tackled one of the crooks and kicked him in the back, causing them all to flee empty-handed.

JAPAN: *The headline read "He may have a tough time in prison."* A polite would- be robber in Ogori city, asked permission to rob a convenience store – and when the clerk told him to get lost, the fellow turned himself in to police.

JAPAN: *The headline read: "Son in chopstick slay."* Aa Japanese man was arrested after admitting to killing his elderly father with a chopstick. Michikazu Ikeuchi, 51, said he stabbed his 80-year-old father in the throat with the wooden utensil after a fight broke out in their Osaka home. Ikeuchi told police that he had tried to stop his parents from arguing and he did not intend to kill his father but said he was angry when he waved the chopstick in front of his father, and before he knew it, it got stuck in him. The chopstick was a foot long, used mostly for cooking. He called police immediately after the incident. No report on whether charges will be brought against the son.

JAPAN: *Phony lion?* Workers at a zoo in the Ehime Prefecture chased and captured a person wearing a furry lion costume during a rare escape drill. Footage from Tobe Zoological Park shows the fake lion happily walking around on two legs – before staffers pull up in a van and toss a net over him.

MEXICO: *Body recovered.* A man stole a car after seeing the keys dangling in the ignition. However, it turned out to be a hearse with a dead body inside. Police in Tlaquepaque say Annibal Saul, 40, stole the vehicle while it was waiting to transport the corpse of an 80-year-old man from a hospital to a funeral home. They caught him on a highway, and both the car and the body were recovered.

NEW ZEALAND: *They swiped the whole thing!* A thief took burglary to a new level when he swiped a couple's entire tiny house. Bianca Balducci and her partner Stephen had nearly completed building the insulated 24-by-8-foot white abode in Auckland when the bandit rolled away with it on a trailer bed truck.

RUSSIA: *The headline read: "Small wonder, "I'd add – OUCH!* A Russian man lopped off his best friend's penis with an axe after their penis-measuring contest. The two middle-aged men had been binge drinking when they pulled out their members and a measuring tape to settle an argument about whose was the longest. The smaller man, then in a rage, sliced off his friend's member. So much for friendship!

RUSSIA: The headline read, "Russian spying is for the birds." Allegedly, Russia's military unveiled a drone designed to look like a huge snowy owl with a wingspan of five feet, aimed at getting closer to targets than regular drones can.

RUSSIA: *In this case the police cannot get behind the behind!* Russian police admit that they cannot get "behind" neighbors upset with a woman who enjoys sun-tanning her rear end – by sticking her legs out of an open second floor window and exposing her bare buttocks. Police in Novosibirsk say they cannot force someone to cover up when they are still technically inside their own home.

PARAGUAY: *DODO DUPITY DUPE POLICE!* We learn that police in Paraguay were duped by thieves who snatched dozens of their rifles and replaced them with plastic toy guns. It took several weeks for officers to begin investigating what happened to the 42 weapons which were set to be replaced with newer ones before they were swiped from a police armory in the town of Capiata. Local media called it "the most embarrassing scandal" in the police force's history.

SOUTH AFRICA: *The "Terminator" gets a kick from a wacko?* A crazed man blasted Arnold Schwarzenegger with a flying double kick to the back one Saturday in May 2019 during a sports events for school children in Johannesburg. Moments before the incident the suspect had walked up behind the 71 Schwarzenegger and waved in an attempt to get the former bodybuilder's attention. A security guard grabbed the man by his arm and led him away, but moments later the man somehow got past the guards and attacked "Arnold" with a flying kick to his back. Schwarzenegger got right back up and assured the crowd that he was OK.

UNITED KINGDOM: *Buns with your beer, perhaps?* It has been reported that one of London's oldest pubs is set to become the city's first nudist bar. Norman's Coach & Horses, which was founded in 1847, received a license to host nude events, complete with naked piano sing-alongs and vegan food.

UNITED KINGDOM: *The headline read, "Her excuse blows."* We learn that a beautician pulled over for drunken driving in England claimed she couldn't take a Breathalyzer test for medical reasons: because her collagen lip implants were too big. Scarlett Harrison, 20, who had been drinking gin with pals in Manchester, reportedly said her plastic pout made it too tough to get her mouth around the blow tube. She was arrested anyway.

UNITED KINGDOM: *Longtime double life!* We learn that a British woman was married for 64 years thinking her spouse was an engineer – but actually he had a secret life as a spy for England since the age of 13. The wife, Audrey Phillips, 85, learned her husband Glyn had been recruited by British Intelligence when he was pulled out of school in 1944 because he had a photographic memory. He was used to overhear Nazi war prisoners' plans plotting against the Brits.

UNITED KINGDOM: *They say her wedding cake came with a side of buns.* We learn that recently a British man proposed to his girlfriend by dropping his pants and flashing a "marry me" tattoo on his behind. Dustin Marshall pulled the gesture after a game of pool with his betrothed. His backside tramp stamp featured a cat's face and the phrase, "Will you marry meow?" She said, "fur sure!"

UNITED KINGDOM: *A brawl over a duck?* We learn that two British simpletons ran afoul of the law when they got into a brawl over a duck in McDonald's. Lee Gaudoin, 31, and Neil Edwards, 40, began bickering with each other over what to do about the duck who had wandered in the restaurant. The bickering turned into a fight with each man taking swings at the other in the town of Chester, police said. When the police showed up to break up the fight, Gaudoin allegedly lashed out an officer and was arrested. The duck waddled out of the premises and no charges were brought against it.

UNITED KINGDOM: *Heartbroken?* A Briton heartbroken after his wife of 35 years left him placed a special sex-doll order. He wants one made that looks exactly like her.

UNITED KINGDOM: *"No Use crying over spilled wine," read the headline.* We learn that a waiter at an upscale British steakhouse found out that when he served a rare French wine that cost $5,700 to a diner who had ordered a wine that cost only $330. The restaurant had to eat the cost and the owner did not fire the waiter. He is giving her a second chance.

UNITED KINGDOM: *How to get potholes filled!* Residents of the English town of Middlesbrough found a great way to persuade officials to fill potholes. How? One or more residents painted penises around every pothole, shaming political leaders into making certain the job was done. The potholes – which had gone unfilled for a year – were fixed within days.

THE END

About the Author

Professor Birdsong received his J.D. from the Harvard Law School and his B.A. from Howard University. He teaches law in Orlando, Florida.

After graduation from law school he worked four years at the law firm of Baker Hostetler. He then entered into a varied and distinguished career in government service. He served as a diplomat with the U.S. State Department with various postings in Nigeria, Germany and the Bahamas.

Professor Birdsong later served as a federal prosecutor. After leaving government service, and before he began teaching, Professor Birdsong was in private law practice in Washington, D.C.

www.BirdsongLaw.com

lbirdsong22@gmail.com

Ordering Information

New books coming soon!

Dear Reader,

If you liked this book, I would greatly appreciate you writing me a review on Amazon or any other book site.

I look forward to sharing more funny stories with you in future books.

Thank you, I really appreciate your help.

Regards,

Professor Birdsong

Winghurst Publications
1969 S. Alafaya Trail / Suite 303
Orlando, FL 32828-8732
www.BirdsongLaw.com
lbirdsong22@gmail.com

Books by
Professor Birdsong:

- Professor **Birdsong**'s 77 Dumbest Criminals Stories (Kindle & Paperback)

- Professor Birdsong's 147 Dumbest Criminal Stories: Florida (Kindle)

- Professor Birdsong's 157 Dumbest Criminal Stories (Kindle & Paperback)

- Professor Birdsong's Weird Criminal Law Stories (Kindle)

- Professor Birdsong's "365" Weird Criminal Law Stories for Every Day of the Year (Kindle)

- Professor Birdsong's Weird Criminal Law Stories, Volume 2: Stories From Around the States and Abroad (Kindle)

- Professor Birdsong's Weird Criminal Law Stories, Volume 3: Stories From New York City and the East Coast. (Kindle)

- Professor Birdsong's Weird Criminal Law Stories - Volume 4: Stories from the Midwest (Kindle)

- Professor Birdsong's Weird Criminal Law Stories, Volume 5: Stories from Way Out West (Kindle)

- Professor Birdsong's Weird Criminal Law Stories - Volume 6: Women in Trouble (Kindle)

- Professor Birdsong's Weird Criminal Law - Volume 6: Women in Trouble! (Paperback)

- Professor Birdsong's LAW SCHOOL GUIDE: Techniques for Choosing and Applying to Law School

- Professor Birdsong's: IMMIGRATION: Obama must act now!

- Professor Birdsong's 157 Dumbest Thieves

- Professor Birdsong's 157 Dumbest Thugs

- Professor Birdsong's 177 Dumbest Rogues

www.ingramcontent.com/pod-product-compliance
Lightning Source LLC
Chambersburg PA
CBHW021209020426
42331CB00003B/271